THE UNEMPLOYMENT GUIDE

How A Setback Can Launch Your Career

By Melissa Fleury

DEDICATION

Thank you, God, for trusting me with this message to deliver to Your people. I've been through a lot and in this moment, I know that it was worth it, Romans 8:28.

To my family and friends who have constantly encouraged me to get this book done, I thank you for the push that I needed. Your support has carried me through the moments when I wanted to quit.

To Mommy and Papi, you've raised a daughter that will change the legacy of our family.

This is only the beginning.

CONTENTS

James 1·2-4 The Message (MSG)
Faith Under Pressure

²⁻⁴Consider it a sheer gift, friends, when tests and challenges come at you from all sides. You know that under pressure, your faith-life is forced into the open and shows its true colors. So don't try to get out of anything prematurely. Let it do its work so you become mature and well-developed, not deficient in any way.

INTRODUCTION

No one ever imagines themselves unemployed. We know that it's a possibility, but we never think that it could happen to us. What do you do when the job that you have given your best efforts, tells you that you're no longer needed? Or when one mistake costs you a career that you've worked so hard to build? Or you studied hard, wrote a phenomenal résumé, obtained a degree from the best school and the only job you can find is paying a yearly salary less than your total student loan debt. Unemployment seems to affect us all whether it's you, your spouse, family or a friend. It's not only financially stressful, but also emotionally and psychologically draining.

If you've picked up this book then I know that you're going through a tough time. When I was laid off from my employer, I wasn't sure where my next steps would lead me. Aside from finding a new job, I knew I had to be financially responsible with what little I had. Then, I had all of this free time that I refused to waste by lying on the couch. I knew that I finally had my opportunity to press the reset button on my life and I was going to take full advantage of it. I wanted a new career, but the outdated advice from my college career center wouldn't help. I found myself in uncharted territory, trying to create a game plan from scratch.

I wrote this book because it has all the things I needed during my time of unemployment. I needed clarity for my career and finances, but most importantly, a vision for the person that I wanted to become. I have included some thought-provoking questions that I hope you will take the time to answer as well as worksheets to clearly create a road map to get you through. I have also included survival tips to guide you along your journey.

I can't tell you how long this period will last for you; however, I'm here to help you manage your way through it.

CHAPTER ONE

IT'S NOT YOU, IT'S ME

It was a normal day when I arrived at work. I sat at my desk, organized my to-do list and put on my headphones, listening to the Miseducation of Lauryn Hill. The first song on the album, Lost Ones, was mid-track when I received an email about an impromptu meeting. I walked into the meeting room not thinking anything out of the norm, but when I opened the door and saw my manager with a pamphlet in front of him. I knew what was happening.

I sat down at the conference table and my manager began to explain that the department was downsizing. He reaffirmed that I hadn't done anything wrong, it was "just the market." My manager gave me a look of remorse and told me he'd be happy to be a referral for any position I applied to. I tried my best to give him a genuine smile, but it still stung that they were letting me go. I know it's prideful, but I wanted to be in control of when I decided to leave the company.

It was a weird out of body experience. On one hand, I couldn't believe this was happening to me, yet at the same time I was relieved. I had been in my role with no growth for a few years and it was wearing me out. I wasn't, however, motivated enough to change my situation because the pay was decent enough for me to stay. Maybe you were like me; you stayed because you were unsure if you could find another job. Perhaps, you feared going through a learning curve and being challenged by the work of a new job. Or possibly procrastination got the best of you and you kept putting off updating your résumé.

Although uncomfortable, my current job was all I knew for the past six years. I was comfortable in my discomfort. I was miserable and knew that I couldn't fully explore my potential and gifts if I stayed there. In spite of this, I was still lax and lacked urgency to find a new job. Once I received my "it's not you, it's me" papers, things became very urgent. Here I was in Dallas, alone with a small severance package and even smaller savings account with big decisions to make.

Tons of questions raced through my mind. Would I stay in Dallas or move back home to New York? How long would it take me to find a job? Should I switch careers now? How will I pay my bills? In the midst of the panic I knew that things would work in my favor. I wasn't sure how and I definitely wasn't sure when, but I began to act as if it were so. At that moment, I felt something I hadn't felt in a long time; peace. It would be something that I would hold on to during this time.

I walked back to my desk and instantly regretted the number of things on and in it. I made my desk comfortable, maybe too comfortable. I was throwing away the rest of my belongings while trying to keep the tears of disappointment at bay. In that moment, not having a job makes you feel like a failure. I thought I did everything right, I went to school, and I worked for an amazing company. I finished clearing my desk, handed in my badge and left my job of six years for good.

When I arrived home, I started the painful task of giving my close friends and family the news. Everyone was shocked, and each time I had to retell the story of being called into that meeting room I felt as if my wounds of shame were opening again and again. I relived that moment until I made the decision to stop retelling the story until it didn't make me feel so raw and exposed.

I purposefully didn't tell some close family and friends because I knew they would make me worry more than I needed to. I was aware that I didn't have a job and my bills needed to be paid, but reminding me of my situation would not pay my bills any sooner. I knew that they loved me, but reiterating the stress of the unknowns would not help my current position. Until I was mentally and emotionally strong enough to manage my unemployment, I continued business as usual.

To be honest, the real reason why I couldn't talk about my layoff was that I was disappointed in myself, my career, my finances, my personal life and with my body (comfort tends to show itself on your waistline). I was disappointed because this moment showed me that I had nothing. The crazy thing is that when you have nothing, you start to realize that you can have everything. I mean, what else do you have to lose? When you're already at the bottom, where else can you go?

Questions for Reflection·

What were your initial emotions and reactions when you became unemployed?

If you were unsatisfied with your job, why did you stay so long even though you were miserable?

What areas of your life are you comfortable with although you know you're ready for a change?

CHAPTER TWO

THE MORNING AFTER

18Forget the things that happened in the past. Do not keep on thinking about them. 19I am about to do something new. It is beginning to happen even now. Don't you see it coming? I am going to make a way for you to go through the desert. I will make streams of water in the dry and empty land.
Isaiah 43: 18-19 NIRV

We will soon begin building out your career plan, but first, let's discuss creating your identity. I woke up the next day at my normal weekday time with no job to rush to. Going to work was such a big part of my routine; I wasn't sure what to do with my free time. Yes, I would apply to jobs but what else would I do? Creating a new routine was hard, but what was even more difficult were the awkward conversations. I no longer had a response to give when someone would ask me "what do you do?"

Whether I liked my job or not, it still felt good that I was perceived as a "responsible" adult in society with a career. I feared that while unemployed, people would view me as lazy, lacking skill and motivation. I knew that wasn't true, however, I couldn't shake that insecurity or the reality that my job validated me. Let's be honest, we live in a culture where people assign a level of respect and judgment towards you based on your career.

Who am I without a job? In an extreme case, if I never find a job, who is Melissa? I know that I'm extremely passionate about excellence; I'm brilliant, compassionate, creative, giving, a problem solver, and a comedian. So what does this have to do with unemployment? Well...everything. This will not be the only hurdle or disappointment you will face in life. Your reaction or how you deal with things will depend on the strength of the foundation of who you are. If you do not know who that person is, this is the perfect opportunity to discover or create that person.

I realized that a huge part of my confidence is that I felt validated by the image of having it all together. When my job was eliminated, it forced me to take inventory of who I was no matter what situation I was placed in. I needed to assign my own labels and redefine myself based on who I was created to be. The only problem: who in the world was that person?

I found who I was by digging into my faith. I read and studied scripture casually for a long time, but when difficult times emerged, I began to search for deep, intimate significance in the Bible. My favorite bible verse is Romans 8:28. "And we know that all things work together for the good to those who love God, and to those who are called according to His purpose." All things work together; the good, the bad, the highs, the lows; they all work together for your good.

Many times I would say "Oh I trust God, it's all about His will and not mine," but faith only works when you relinquish control. And in this situation, I had no control. I submitted to a belief and a plan that if I could get through this time, not matter how painful it might be, I would come out a better person. Maybe, just maybe this period of my life is much bigger than losing a job. There was more out there for me to see, to do, and to experience. Possibly, this was about plucking me from my comfort zone and developing my faith muscle to receive and be an awesome steward over something else.

SURVIVAL TIP

Your friends and family will probably tell you to "have faith." But you're probably thinking, 'Sallie Mae and your mortgage company cannot use faith as a form of payment.' It's true they can't. But you're already feeling as if you're in the lowest part of your life. What do you have to lose by choosing to believe that "maybe this could all work out for my good?"

Close your eyes, take a deep breath, and imagine what life looks like on the other side of unemployment. Faith is believing in something that you can't tangibly see but knowing that it will come to fruition. Give yourself permission to dream like a child again. On the next page, write down your uninhibited vision for your life.

THE UNEMPLOYMENT GUIDE

CHAPTER THREE

THE POWER OF PRAYER

⁸Keep this Book of the Law always on your lips; meditate on it day and night, so that you may be careful to do everything written in it. Then you will be prosperous and successful. Joshua 1·8 NIV

I was a committed church member attending services on Sunday and Bible study on Wednesday, but my prayer life wasn't the greatest. I substituted my acts of service in ministry instead of developing an intimate relationship with God. I thought that as long as I did the things that "good" Christians were supposed to do, then I had a strong relationship with God. I soon learned that I personally knew nothing about the great God that I proclaimed to love. I made excuses for spending time with God, whether through prayer, meditation, or journaling because I had to work. I would try to convince myself that I never had "enough time" and that God "knew my heart." Besides, I wasn't a "bad" person, so He would understand.

And it is impossible to please God without faith. Anyone who wants to come to him must believe that God exists and that he rewards those who sincerely seek him.
Hebrews 11·6 NLT

I now had more than enough time to seek God, but I struggled with how to do it? The word "seek" is a verb and by definition it means to attempt to find something. I soon learned that in order to develop a relationship with God it had to be intentional and filled with action.

I have always been an avid writer, so I began journaling my prayers, thoughts, and feelings. The best times, I found, was early in the morning or before I went to bed. I went back to the basics of creating a relationship with God. I was childlike in my pursuit in learning Christ, and I approached this new relationship as if I knew nothing about Him at all.

I believed in Christ and the works that He performed in the New Testament. I believed that He died on the cross to gift the world salvation and eternal life. But as I continued to journal, I realized that my belief was that God's promise was for everyone else and not for me. For years I had been comparing my life and accomplishments to those of my peers.

I felt that since things weren't "happening" for me then maybe the scriptures where He promised abundance, joy, and peace weren't for me. However, I never considered that confidence, faith and steadfastness were directly tied to my connection to God. That my life was a result of the things that I didn't ask for and the negative words that I spoke over myself. "Good things like that don't ever happen for me," or "I wasn't meant to have those things" and "I will never be happy." I stopped dreaming and settled on a reality instead of seeking what God intended for me to do. I considered these:

Words kill, words give life; they're either poison or fruit
you choose.
Proverbs 18·21 MSG

So let us come boldly to the throne of our gracious God.
There we will receive his mercy, and we will find grace to
help us when we need it most.
Hebrews 4·16 NLT

Because of Christ and our faith in him, we can now come
boldly and confidently into God's presence.
Ephesians 3·12 NLT

Boldness was something that I was lacking. As uncomfortable as it was, I was raw and honest in my prayers with God. The things that I once wrote in my journal, I began to say them aloud to God during my quiet time and devotion.

"But from there you will seek the LORD your God, and
you will find Him if you search for Him with all your
heart and all your soul."
Deuteronomy 4·29 AMP

The message translation of Deuteronomy 4:29 puts it this way: "But even there, if you seek God, your God, you'll be able to find him if you're serious, looking for him with your whole heart and soul. When troubles come and all these awful things happen to you, in future days you will come back to GOD, your God, and listen obediently to what he says. GOD, your God, is above all a compassionate God. In the end he will not abandon you, he won't bring you to ruin, he won't forget the covenant with your ancestors which he swore to them."

THE RENEWAL PROCESS

Renewing your mind is a daily process. Romans 12:2 says, "Do not be conformed to the pattern of this world but be transformed by the renewing of your mind. Then you will be able to test and approve what God's will is—his good, pleasing and perfect will." You must be willing to admit that you didn't do all the right things at your job. Maybe you were late on so many occasions that you can't even count. Or perhaps admitting that the job you prayed for lost its sparkle after a few months and you stopped bringing your best self a long time ago.

Renewing your mind means taking accountability for the person you were but being intentional about creating a better future version of yourself. You'll have to constantly examine your thoughts and learn how to manage your feelings. I once heard that you must "think about what you're thinking about." Your thoughts will guide everything you do and ultimately will manifest itself in your life. If your thoughts aren't encouraging you, pushing you forward or demanding that you bring the best version of yourself every day, then it cannot take up residence in your mind. Do not give negative thoughts the space to grow roots.

SURVIVAL TIP

A good friend of mine once told me "the world only gives you a day." Meaning that people allow you a short period of sympathy when difficult situations arise. You're allowed to be mad, sad, angry and disappointed, but the expectation is that you'll learn how to move on. You cannot stay in a rut, nor can you expect others to sympathize with you for long periods of time. Make the decision to mentally shift gears and work against the daily negative thoughts of doubt that inundate your mind. I am not discrediting your feelings nor implying that it's not valid, but will you make the decision to give yourself the opportunity to think differently?

Here are some scriptures you can reference daily to renew your mind:

My flesh and my heart fail; but God is the strength of my heart and my portion forever
Psalms 73:26 NKJV

So teach us to number our days, that we may gain a heart of wisdom
Psalms 90:12 NKJV

So do not fear, for I am with you; do not be dismayed, for I am your God. I will strengthen you and help you; I will uphold you with my righteous right hand
Isaiah 41:10 NIV

The Lord and King helps me. He won't let me be dishonored. So, I've made up my mind to keep on serving Him. I know He won't let me be put to shame.
Isaiah 50·7 NIRV

[28]Come to Me, all of you who are tired and are carrying heavy loads. I will give you rest. [29]Become my servants and learn from me. I am gentle and free of pride. You will find rest for your souls. [30]Serving me is easy, and my load is light.
Matthew 11·28-30 NIRV

[11]And we desire that each one of you show the same diligence to the full assurance of hope until the end, [12]that you do not become sluggish, but imitate those who through faith and patience inherit the promises.
Hebrews 6·11-12 NKJV

After you have suffered for a little while, the God of all grace [who imparts His blessing and favor], who called you to His own eternal glory in Christ, will Himself complete, confirm, strengthen, and establish you [making you what you ought to be].
1 Peter 5·10 AMP

WHAT WILL BE YOUR TESTIMONY?

There's something powerful about having an impactful testimony, and that means going through a test. We seem to want the victory of the war but don't want to fight the battles. Some of these tests are our own doing, however, it's not about the things that happen to you, it's about your response to it. Did you complain the entire time? Were you prideful and refused to ask for help? Can you admit that sometimes it was difficult to encourage yourself to be productive with your day?

No other person is responsible for your success but you. I've dealt with difficult bosses and coworkers, but they are not to blame for my layoff. We have the tendency to place blame on others when things happen to us. We shift the spotlight and energy onto someone else, when we could use the time to make ourselves better. Release what others have done, or didn't do, and create the opportunity to live differently.

Your impact starts when you begin to take responsibility for your actions. Our mistakes don't make us weak; they make us human. Your testimony through your unemployment will inspire others that difficult times don't have to break us. Difficult times create the atmosphere for God to show His miraculous power and glory.

Questions for Reflection·

Describe your current prayer life? What can you do to renew your relationship with God?

What are some limiting beliefs you have about yourself and your ability to be successful?

What would you lose by trusting and having faith in God?

What are your strengths? What are your weakness? What are some things that you'd like to improve upon during this time?

What false identity about yourself do you have trouble releasing?

CHAPTER FOUR

The Financial Strategy

"It's impossible to map out a route to your destination if you don't know where you're starting from." – **Suze Orman**

As you continue to work on your mindset, let's talk about money. It was probably the first thought to come to mind once you received your notice of layoff. It is important to know where you stand financially. Understanding the amount of money flowing in and out of your account will be key to your success in creating a new career path. For me, the reality was that I was unsure of when I would have an income again. I had a working budget I used prior to my layoff, however, I wanted to ensure that I captured every minute detail.

You'll need to collect every single statement and bill that you owe and write them all down on paper. Now is not the time to be in denial about your financial health. If you owe it, put it down on paper and stop relying on rough estimates.

Here's an outline of some major monthly expenses.

Expenses	
Line Item	**Amount**
Housing (Mortgage, Rent, etc)	
Homeowner's/Renter's Insurance	
Utilities (Water, Electric, Heating/Cooling)	
Internet & Cable	
Car Payment/Public Transportation	
Car Insurance	
Gas/Maintenance	
Groceries	
Debt (Credit Cards, Student Loans, Personal Loans, etc)	
Phone Bill	
Giving & Charity	
Insurance (Life, Health, Dental, etc)	
MISC/Other	
MISC/Other	
MISC/Other	
Total Monthly Expenses	

There are fixed expenses that you cannot change such as your housing or your car payment. However, it's imperative to begin reducing or eliminating some of your variable expenses as soon as possible. For example, cable is an expense you can get rid of. There are many streaming services you can use such as Netflix and Hulu. Your grocery bill is another item where you can save money. If you're like me, I was and still am a foodie. I just couldn't justify spending $20 on shrimp at the supermarket anymore. Creating a budget will help you say "no" to the things that will not bring you closer to your goals.

Next, I contacted all my creditors and student loan servicers to discuss my options due to my unemployment. Many creditors offer hardship programs, which will reduce or delay your monthly payments. Federal student loans offer deferment and forbearance options if you qualify. A deferment is when you temporarily suspend your monthly payments. A forbearance will allow you to suspend or reduce your monthly payment. Whether you are responsible for paying the interest accrued will depend on the type of loan you have during your deferment or forbearance. If you have private student loans, your options may be limited, however, still discuss what is available to you during your unemployment.

Be honest about your financial situation as many creditors are willing to work with you to avoid default. Create a budget where you're at least meeting the minimum payment. And if it is not a dire survival need (food, water, etc.) stop utilizing with your credit card.

SURVIVAL TIP

To organize your bills, use a calendar to write down the due date of payment for each expense. Many of us estimate when our bills are due, however, while unemployed it is best to be exact. This is important because some creditors or expenses will allow you to change your due date, which will provide more flexibility with your income. For example, it may be easier to pay your car insurance on the 10th instead of the 28th of the month when three other major expenses are due on that date.

Use this calendar and write down each expense due date. For example, rent due on the 1st of the month, electric on the 4th, internet/cable on the 11th, etc. I personally like to use a calendar so I can visually see which bills are due and when.

Month						
1	2	3	4	5	6	
7	8	9	10	11	12	13
14	15	16	17	18	19	20
21	22	23	24	25	26	27
28	29	30	31			

Making Tough Financial Decisions

I knew that I wanted to make a career switch and that it would take some time for it to happen. After combing through my bills, I knew my largest expense was rent. I made the tough decision to move back home to my parents' basement. A large part of my hesitancy to do so was my pride and ego. I felt like a failure having to come back home and start all over. When I graduated college, I was self-sufficient and now having to ask for help was hard. But once I had the conversation, my parents were more than receptive to me coming back home.

I soon accepted that it was the best decision I made. I knew my fixed expenses like housing and other things could easily exhaust my severance in three months and unemployment would barely cover my expenses past that. Moving in with my parents, however, allowed me to sustain for nine months.

Financial pressures and fears can also cause you to make premature decisions. You'll apply for any job (there is nothing wrong with that), just to meet your immediate fears and needs but you'll be discontent in the long run. You'll end up working another you job you hate with a different employer. I know you're thinking "the point is to find a new job quickly." This is true, but if you've invested in this book then you're probably seeking a change. You owe yourself the opportunity to change your life, so don't short change yourself by going back to what's familiar.

I sold most of my belongings on online marketplaces such as Let Go, Offer Up, and Poshmark. I then submitted ads to sublet my apartment. When that didn't work, I made the decision to break my lease and used the money from sold furniture to pay for the fees associated with it. With my clothes, shoes, and ninja blender (I wasn't letting that go), I moved back home to my old room.

Questions for Reflection.

What are some expenses you can decrease or eliminate?

How will you determine what you should keep or sell?

What are some extra items you're holding onto that could be sold for extra cash?

Organizing Your Sources of Income

Now that we've discussed expenses, let's talk about income. It was important to me to keep as much cash as possible. In the event of an emergency, I wanted to be able to cover any unexpected costs. In this chapter, I will discuss four sources of income: severance, savings, unemployment income and retirement income.

Severance

I was fortunate that when I was laid-off I was given a severance package. A severance package is pay and benefits an employee receives when they are involuntarily terminated. Pay and benefits may include payment of wages based on length of service, payment of unused accrued PTO (vacation, holiday, sick leave, etc), extended health benefits, and outplacement assistance.

My severance was a decent amount; however, I knew it wouldn't last long. A severance package is typically 2-4 weeks' pay for every year worked with a company and is distributed as a lump sum or over time. Companies are not required to provide severance packages to employees they choose to terminate. If you were eligible to receive a severance package, it should include details such as your notice period, severance amount, distribution of paid time off and information on benefits continuation.

If you do not understand the details of your severance package, reach out to your human resource point of contact with your questions.

Savings

Your savings account is for unexpected situations such as this. Your savings can assist you through unemployment until you can replace your income. It's suggested to have approximately 3-6 months' worth of expenses in your savings account. However, if you're like me, then you had maybe one month's worth of expenses and the ability to buy a pack of gum with your savings account. No matter how small or large the amount, keep a frugal mindset and hold onto the money in your account for as long as you can.

Every purchase adds up, so determine what is a necessity and have the discipline to say no to things that are not a part of your financial plan. Maybe you can no longer buy a daily cup of Starbucks coffee or purchase something simply because it's on sale. You'll need to be mindful of every purchase because your career game plan depends on it. Review your bank transactions if not daily, but at minimum a weekly basis.

Unemployment (UE) Benefits

There is typically a waiting period in which you need to be unemployed before you can apply for benefits. On average, the waiting period is one to two-weeks from your date of unemployment. Once I received my severance pay, I immediately applied. Please note that many states allow you to receive unemployment income in addition to your severance pay. Read through your state's unemployment guidelines carefully and speak with a representative from your state's department of labor unemployment office for additional information.

I was eligible to receive unemployment income. I reported all income that I received and was approved by my state. The unemployment process takes a few weeks from the time you apply. After review and approval, you will receive your first benefit deposit. Typically, you're eligible for unemployment income (1) as long as your termination was not your fault, i.e. you did not quit or you were fired, (2) you meet the state's requirement for wages earned for time worked. It is mandatory to report any and all income received during your period of unemployment.

Once approved for unemployment, determine if you want to withhold taxes from your unemployment benefit. I decided not to withhold taxes, which meant that I would pay taxes at the end of the year. However, you should consult a tax professional to discuss which option is best for you.

Unemployment income is normally distributed on a weekly basis for up to 26 weeks. I was accustomed to receiving my pay on a semi-monthly basis. To calculate how much unemployment income, you would receive per month use this basic formula below:

(Weekly UE Amount X 52)/12 = Monthly UE Benefit

For example, if you were approved to receive $420 per week, you would use the formula as follows:

($420 x 52)/12 = $1,820 per month

Depending on the state you're filing in, you may need to meet job search minimums. The state wants to ensure that you are actively searching for employment and not collecting "free" money. At the time of my unemployment, I was working and living in the state of Texas, which requires a minimum of three searches per week. You must keep track of your job search process, because at any moment the state can request proof of your search. I created a job search log as well as copies of my submissions to jobs I applied to.

In addition, some states offer "self-employment assistance programs," which allows you to collect unemployment insurance benefits while you start a business. For instance, the state of New York permits you to work full-time on your new business while collecting unemployment insurance benefits. You do not have to search for jobs while you work on your business. Money earned from your business is not deducted from your unemployment insurance benefits and they assist your success with training and counseling (Self-Employment Assistance Program).

401K/403B/IRA Retirement Withdrawals

Withdrawing funds from your retirement account should be your last and final option. The purpose of your retirement account is to provide means for you to support yourself after you reach retirement age. In addition, using money from this account can result in penalties and taxable income. However, many retirement accounts qualify unemployment as a "hardship" event and may allow you to withdraw funds. If your company plan allows hardship withdrawals, you can find circumstances that qualify under the IRS guidelines. In addition, speak to a financial or investment advisor.

Calculating Unemployment Duration

Once you've gathered all your income information and monthly expenses, you can use the chart below to calculate how many months you can meet your financial obligations. This table will help calculate the length of time your current income could sustain you during unemployment.

Source of Income	Amount
Net (after taxes) Severance Amount	
Total Approved Unemployment Amount (Weekly UE Amount x Max Weekly Duration)	
Current Total Savings and Checking Account Balance	
Total Income	
Total Monthly Expenses (insert figure from previous expense worksheet)	

For example, you received a net severance pay of $7,000. Your state has approved you to receive a weekly unemployment benefit amount of $420 for a maximum of 26 weeks. Your current combined checking and savings account balance is $2,000. Your total monthly expenses are $2,800.

Source of Income	Amount
Net Severance Amount	*$7,000*
Total Approved Unemployment Amount (Weekly UE Amount x Max Weekly Duration)	*$10,920* *($420 x 26)*
Current Total Savings and Checking Account Balance	*$2,000*
Total Income	$7,000+$10,920+ $2,000=$19,920
Total Monthly Expenses	$2,800

You will then take your total income and divide it by your total monthly expenses to calculate how long you can cover your monthly expenses with your current income.

Total Income	
Total Monthly Expenses	
Approximate Months of Unemployment (rounded down)	

Using our example above, your total calculated income is $19,920 and your total monthly expenses are $2,800. Using the chart provided, you can cover seven months of unemployment with your current income.

Total Income	$19,920
Total Monthly Expenses	$2,800
Approximate Months of Unemployment	7 months

It is essential to be conservative with the numbers that you're using. Life will continue to happen and throw you curveballs while you're unemployed. You may have unexpected expenses that you'll need to cover.

CHAPTER FIVE

THE CAREER PATH

[16]A man's gift makes room for him, and brings him before great men.
Proverbs 18·16 NKJV

We all dream of a career that we're passionate about and fulfills us to our core. However, many of us are not working in a place or in a capacity that reflects our gifts. More than likely you were working for a company that was too small for your gifts and talents. Your only motivation to go to work was a paycheck, and that was miserable for you. You now have the space and time to create an opportunity where you can utilize your talents. You should be in an environment where you can be authentic every day. It's hard pretending to be someone else eight plus hours a day, five days a week.

When you would sit at your desk and daydream, where did your thoughts take you? Did you imagine yourself working in a role where you could be creative through design? Has technology been an industry that you've desired to be a part of? Or maybe you wanted to completely switch careers but didn't know how. I want to tell you a story about Danielle.

Danielle obtained her bachelor's degree in business administration and post-graduation, she joined a top investment bank as an analyst. She had a wonderful experience and made great money, but year after year she found herself unhappy. She started to take inventory of the things that brought her joy.

She reflected on her senior year in college when she took a women's health class focused on reproductive health and infantile care. She remembered how intrigued she was in class and even considered becoming a medical professional. She watched how the doctors provided such care for their patients, and it inspired her to want to do the same in other women's lives.

She lacked the education needed to apply for a health science graduate program and besides; she already had a career in finance. The thought of having to "start over" kept her in her analyst position longer than she should have. She decided to take a science class at a local community college to see if she could invest in her dream full-time.

Unexpectedly during the semester, Danielle was laid off from her job. She was so relieved because she now had the opportunity to pursue a dream that she thought was unattainable. It turns out, starting over was the best thing that could have happened to her. She continued taking science classes to prepare herself to apply to a Physician's Assistant program. She accepted a position as a doctor's assistant to fund her education and obtain the experience necessary for her application. She has completed her second year in a top PA program and is preparing to graduate.

When creating your career plan, you need to decide if you want to stay in the same career or switch the industry and/or functions entirely. These two paths will require different tactics and timelines. Finding a job in your current industry and function may be quicker to accomplish once you've updated your résumé, professional online profile, and created a networking strategy (we'll talk more on this).

My professional experience is in underwriting and risk management. Initially, I made the decision to remain within that same function and industry and applied to jobs looking for my particular skill set. I found myself interviewing for positions within a month of my layoff. I was offered a role with great benefits and an OK salary. I weighed my pros and cons over whether I'd accept this new role. I desired to switch industries and transition into commercial real estate. I reviewed my finances and was comfortable knowing I could give myself some time to find the job that I wanted. Although difficult, I declined the offer because it didn't align with where I wanted to take my career. This was my opportunity to bet on myself.

Careers I thought I couldn't transition into now seemed like viable options for me. As I created a career plan, I was aware that I lacked some of the technical skills needed within commercial real estate. I found programs that offered coursework to learn and fill in those gaps. I joined professional organizations centered on real estate, which exposed me to a network of professionals with similar goals.

I was extremely engaged and attended as many events and workshops that I could. Surrounding yourself with people who are in positions you aspire to be in creates an environment where you'll find the clues for success. Through these many events I learned the lingo, the key players in my industry, who was hiring, and met influential people who guided me through my transition.

Many of these programs and events cost money. As I previously discussed in the financial chapter, you need to be as frugal as possible. However, deciding which events and programs are an investment in your career may be a challenge. There are costs associated with attending events such as registration, transportation and food. In addition, educational programs can cost hundreds to thousands of dollars. In my opinion, investing in programs and events that will strengthen your technical skills and expand your network will always be an asset. Before you spend money, research thoroughly and be clear on your end result.

Withstanding the No's

I applied to commercial real estate positions on a daily basis. For months, the only responses I received were the standard automated emails that read "we regret to inform you that we will not move forward with your candidacy." I became frustrated with each rejection, and I felt as if I would never reach my goal. Negative thoughts and feelings multiplied in my mind and led me down a rabbit hole of self-pity and doubt. I would feel down about an interview that didn't' go well and scroll on social media and watch as friends posted smiling pictures enjoying life. I would convince myself that I was the only person with problems and compare my story to a short moment in their life.

Worrying made me restless and at times I became unsure of my plan. When those moments arose, I took my concerns to God through prayer.

⁶Do not be anxious about anything, but in every situation, by prayer and petition, with thanksgiving, present your requests to God. ⁷And the peace of God, which transcends all understanding, will guard your hearts and your minds in Christ Jesus.
Phil 4. 6-7 (NIV)

I created a habit of reflecting on the things I was grateful for. A spirit of gratitude and thanksgiving tends to overshadow feelings of lack, worry, and uneasiness. For me, I was grateful for health, supportive family and friends, the ability to meet my financial obligations, and even the opportunity to pursue my dreams.

With each "no," I strengthened my resiliency muscle. I stopped taking the rejection so personally and viewed it as an opportunity to improve. Many times, when we hear "no" we internalize it and think it's a reflection of our value. The truth is that you are priceless. A recruiter or hiring manager should never have the power to make you feel worthless. Instead, view rejection as an opportunity to improve on your interviewing and presentation skills or simply saving you from a role/company that was not the right fit for you.

I continued to apply to companies and positions that were aligned with my next career move. With one month of unemployment income remaining, I decided to pivot from my plan of finding mid-level commercial real estate roles. I began applying to any position that would get me in the door of the industry. I found a secretarial position at a highly respected real estate investment trust. I figured I could work myself up the company ladder and learn the industry. I submitted my résumé and within an hour, I received a phone call from the recruiter asking me to come in for an interview.

I quickly made my way to the office where the recruiter informed me that he thought I was overqualified for the secretary position. However, after reviewing my résumé he wanted to find me a role at the company because he believed I could add value. That day I interviewed with three different departments and multiple managers and senior executives. I was offered a role as a senior analyst in asset management a month later, which I accepted.

Since my unemployment, I've been able to travel the country working on multi-million-dollar assets and projects, from massive apartment buildings and offices to hotels and coworking spaces. The experience has been amazing, and my career has taken off with increased responsibility, visibility, and a promotion. My end goal never changed, but I've learned to be flexible in the path to get there. Learning to bounce back from disappointment is crucial to your success because you never know when the next opportunity will present itself.

Questions for Reflection

Write down and describe a career that you're interested in but have been putting off.

Are you seeking to find a new job in your current industry or make a career transition?

What are the requirements for the new career you are seeking to pursue?

Will you need additional schooling or certifications?

Where are your professional gaps? (technical skills, years of experienced, education, etc)

Using the chart on the next page, compare the pros and cons of staying in your current line of work or transitioning careers. After reviewing the chart, make a decision to go in the direction you want to pursue. For additional information visit www.thebrandedcareer.com.

CAREER PATH	
CURRENT INDUSTRY/ROLE	
PROS	CONS
NEW INDUSTRY/ROLE	
PROS	CONS

Résumé Revamp

Whether you're looking to remain in the same career or transition careers, you'll need to take inventory of your skill set and where you can add value. Let's begin by looking at your résumé.

Résumés can feel somewhat like a burden. After you've gone through tons of job postings and found the position you really want, you need to sit and craft a résumé to show an employer that you're the best candidate for the position. Your résumé is a professional portfolio of your accomplishments and experiences, which communicate why you're an asset . Your résumé should not read as a job history or description. Instead, it should highlight your accomplishments.

Take the time to reflect on moments where you've made significant contributions to your previous organization. People are impressed by impact, not responsibility. If you choose to stay in the same career industry or function, crafting a résumé will focus mainly on highlighting your accomplishments, impact, as well as any future contributions you will be able to make to the employer. Take the time to list out every major accomplishment you have either been formally recognized for or use your performance evaluations to extract information about what you've achieved. If you work in a service-based business, use client reviews and recommendations when you were recognized for your efforts.

Be as specific as possible when describing your experiences on your résumé. In order to show impact, you'll want to use numbers, specific values, dollar amounts and percentages to display your influence and responsibility. Here are a few examples of how you can change your résumé and create something that will catch the eye of the recruiter.

Before: Provide health and wellness education to students during the school year.

After: Service 450 students during the school year ensuring their health and wellness education needs are successfully met through goal setting, workshops and parental engagement.

Before: Supervises all activities to ensure safety of students at all times.

After: Implement positive classroom management strategies and disciplinary programs to effectively manage challenging behavior and ensuring safety at all times.

Before: Manage and grew a portfolio of business while managing front line sales representatives.

After: Owned a portfolio of approximately $20 million and managed nine front line sales representatives to grow new and existing business through training, coaching and development.

Before: Conducted brainstorming sessions to develop solutions for improving patient services.

After: Spearheaded quarterly brainstorming sessions to develop solutions for improving patient services and identify inefficiencies while making recommendations for process improvements.

Before: Oversee a large portfolio of assets to ensure successful exit of a short-term structured loan.

After: Manage $100MM portfolio of multifamily assets ensuring successful exit of bridge loans through financial analysis, quarterly valuations, and monitoring capital improvement plans.

Create a résumé that specifically conveys to an employer that you would be an asset to the team. Use Google as a resource to research sample résumés for the industry and function that you're applying to. Use these résumés as a reference to see what employers are seeking in a candidate.

If you're having difficulty writing a résumé, consider seeking out a professional. A résumé writer is a professional who assists you with crafting your résumé specific to a job or industry that you're applying to. Résumé writing services can be expensive; however, there are plenty of low-cost alternatives that you can use to find a résumé writer. Websites such as Fiverr (www.fiverr.com) or Upwork (www.upwork.com) are marketplaces where freelancers offer their services. You can search for résumé writing and purchase services for as low as $20. This is a good investment if you're having difficulty revamping your résumé.

In addition to a résumé writer you can also change the template or aesthetic of your résumé. We're currently in a competitive job market and what better way to catch a recruiter's attention than to use a different template? Recruiters typically spend less than 30 seconds reviewing a résumé and a completely different template could cause a recruiter to stop and look at yours even longer. Consider websites such as Etsy (www.etsy.com) or Creative Market (www.creativemarket.com). Simply typing in "résumé template" into the search bar will yield tons of results for you to choose from that are relatively inexpensive.

Key Words and Phrases

The Applicant Tracking System (ATS) is an industry standard software that recruiters and companies use to not only keep track of their recruiting process but also find the best candidate for their job posting using keyword analysis. If your résumé does not contain the keywords they're seeking, more than likely your résumé will be placed into a black hole never to be found again. However, this is advantageous to you because the job requisition shows you exactly how to build a résumé that employers want to see. The job description gives you the keywords and the road map to crafting a résumé, recruiters are looking for.

The skills and experiences listed on your résumé should coincide with the role you are applying to. If you're applying for a finance position are you highlighting your analysis and

Excel skills? If it's a project management position are you using words such as "budget," "scope," and "deliverables" on your résumé? Marketing positions should communicate brand/content planning, sales, and client acquisition successes. Depending on your role, the skills listed will be tailored to your experience. However, you're doing your professional brand a disservice by not being intentional about the skills that showcase your expertise. One the next page is a list of the best résumé words you should use to make yours stand out.

BEST RÉSUMÉ WORDS

Accelerate	Facilitate	Produce
Achieve	Founded	Propose
Advertise	Forecast	Publish
Advocate	Formulate	Qualify
Analyze	Generate	Quantify
Award	Hire	Recommend
Built	Identify	Reconcile
Budget	Improve	Recruit
Campaign	Increase	Reduce
Certify	Influence	Resolve
Coach	Initiate	Restructure
Communicate	Innovate	Simplify
Compose	Integrate	Solved
Consolidate	Launch	Spearhead
Consult	Maintain	Specialize
Chair	Manage	Supervise
Create	Mentor	Surpass
Decrease	Monitor	Sustain
Demonstrate	Motivate	Target
Dedicate	Negotiate	Train
Deliver	Organized	Transact
Efficient	Outperform	Transform
Engineer	Outpaced	Unify
Enhance	Oversaw	Update
Establish	Partnered	Utilize
Evaluate	Planned	Volunteer
Examine	Prioritize	Yield

SURVIVAL TIP

For those interested in making a career switch, I highly recommend working with a career coach, a coaching professional whose sole purpose is to assist you with obtaining your career goals. You'll want to find a career coach that specializes in your needs and who you can connect with. Your coach will only be able to help you as much as you're willing to reveal about your fears, weaknesses and insecurities. A good career coach will be able to help you create a strategy to help you find a job, but a great one will help you overcome limiting beliefs to create a career of your dreams. A career coach is definitely an investment, but like any successful athlete, coaches guide you in your pursuit of success.

Cover Letters

Cover letters are often difficult to write. However, you don't want to miss out on an opportunity because of the effort it takes to write one. Your cover letter doesn't need to be over the top and it shouldn't be a replica of the information on your résumé. I suggest using an achievement from your professional experience and expand upon the who, what, where and how. It gives your cover letter some depth as well as demonstrates why an employer should reach out to you for an interview. Your cover letter is also the place where you can explain career gaps, career transitions or highlight relevant experience/education. You're cover letter can proactively answer the questions your résumé can't.

How to Structure A Cover Letter

Heading. Within the heading you should list the best contact information where a recruiter or hiring manager can reach you. Your heading will include your name, address, phone number and email address. If you haven't already, create a professional email address using your first and last name; for example, janejobseeker@gmail.com. Your contact information should be consistent across your résumé, job application and social media. Next, you'll address the letter directly to the recruiter or hiring manager of the position. If you do not know the name of the hiring manager I suggest using "Dear Hiring Manager," as a last resort if you haven't found their contact online.

First Paragraph. Use the first paragraph of your cover letter to express your interest. Communicate how you found the position whether through the company website, online job board, referral, etc.

Second Paragraph. The second paragraph provides a brief overview of your current position and/or skill set and how it relates to the position you are applying to.

Third Paragraph. The third paragraph expands upon specific projects you've worked on and the result. Show your impact and how you'd be an asset to the prospective group. Use the job opening as a guideline to highlight specific past experiences that are relevant to the role.

Final Paragraph. The last paragraph is a space to talk about your "why" and show the recruiter why you're passionate about the job and why they should choose you for an interview.

Here is a sample cover letter.

Your Name
Your Address
Your City, State, Zip Code
Your Phone Number
Your Email Address

Date

Dear Mr./Ms. Last Name,

I am writing in response to your LinkedIn post for the associate role within the affordable housing real estate group of XYZ Company. As a current analyst for 123 Company, I have a thorough understanding of real estate banking, risk assessment and economic development. I am an ambitious and energetic professional with financial service experience seeking to utilize my skills in real estate.

As an analyst, my primary responsibility is to perform due diligence to ensure that the borrower's expectation of their lending experience has been exceeded. During my time with 123 Company, I have consistently been recognized for my quality work and exceed departmental expectations. To assist with my transition into real estate, I have completed commercial real estate coursework in financing, leasing, asset management and zoning as well as market research and its economic impact on the surrounding community.

I have a passion for community and economic development. I volunteered with a nonprofit called ABC Homes. Their primary goal is to increase homeownership within the low- and moderate-income population. As a coordinator, I increased attendance of workshops by 33%, restructured programming to ensure effective delivery, as well as established relationships with key community members and business owners. My volunteer experience has also exposed me to economic and community development grants required for this role.

I am extremely passionate about producing excellent work and building relationships. I understand that this position entails aligning the business needs of XYZ Company with those of other key stakeholders in the community, and I am confident that I can contribute with my knowledge of the financial industry.

I have enclosed my résumé for your review. I look forward to hearing from you soon regarding this opportunity.

Respectfully,
Signature (hard copy letter)
Jane Jobseeker

LinkedIn

I am a huge advocate of LinkedIn. Many people aren't aware of the resources and power that this platform has to change the trajectory of their career. LinkedIn is a social networking platform for professionals with approximately 500 million users. LinkedIn has several uses such as connecting with colleagues and professionals, displaying your skills and experiences through your profile, as well as a search engine for jobs, just to name a few. LinkedIn is such a great resource; however, you need to actively use it to yield results. It is one of the first channels of social media that recruiters not only use for their talent search but also their research of you. Take the time to craft a profile that represents your professional brand. Here are my keys to optimizing LinkedIn.

Take a professional photo. It's the first thing people see. You don't have to spend much on a headshot. If you don't have access to a professional camera or know a photographer, use your phone. Choose a neutral background, wear your best outfit, and put on your best smile.

Craft a strong summary. In this area of your profile, you can create a bio that establishes your brand, credibility and skills. Within this section you can show your personality. However, I do recommend that you keep it professional. You can showcase your interests and passions, but just like your résumé, your profile should tell a cohesive story. Think of your summary as a place that answers the questions "what do you want to be known for?" For example:

Jane is an established business professional and entrepreneur with experience in financial services. Her technical skills include strong quantitative analysis in project and program management. She has proven success in executing in demanding and deadline driven environments and is always perceived as a highly positive, motivated and a committed team player. She has a passion for transforming people and their communities. She actively engages in mentoring, planning financial literacy programs and most recently, established a consulting firm focused on strategy and project management for emerging nonprofits. Through her work, she hopes to make a lasting impact that will last generations.

Personalize your LinkedIn Profile URL. Your current profile URL is most likely your name and a combination of letters and numbers. Keep it simple and professional and edit the URL to your first and last name. If you're like me and you have a common name, you may need to be a bit more creative if your URL name is taken. For example, your URL should read https://www.LinkedIn.com/in/janejobseeker.

Do not use LinkedIn as a *casual* social media site. What sets LinkedIn apart from other social media platforms is the intention to make professional business connections. Share and create content that is relevant to your professional interests. LinkedIn in not a dating site, so be mindful of your conversations with other professionals.

Connect with professionals you do not personally know. After you have created your profile, start connecting with colleagues, classmates, or clients you may have worked with in the past. The beauty of LinkedIn is that you have access to millions of professionals that work in a career that you desire. I recommend searching for a company that interests you. Within the search results, LinkedIn will display professionals that share the company name within their profile. You'll also see their degree of connection to you, i.e., 1st, 2nd, 3rd. Instead of attempting to connect with the standard "I'd like to join your network" message. Craft a note that is personalized stating why you're reaching out to them and why you'd like to connect.

The purpose of LinkedIn is to create professional connections with others to help advance careers, businesses and professional relationships. However, you may be asking how should you reach out to someone you don't know? Well the great news is that users on LinkedIn are expecting messages and connections from people they don't know. Although, most messages you send may go unanswered, you'll never know unless you try.

I found that strategically using LinkedIn to further my career search was extremely advantageous. Each week, I created a list of 10-15 professionals that I wanted to connect with either in person or on the phone and I received a 1 to 3% response. Once my headshot and professional summary were in place, I began reaching out with the following cold email below.

Hi (First Name),
Thank you for accepting my request to join your LinkedIn network. I am reaching out to you with hopes that I would be able to gain some insight into your career path. I am young within my career and I'm seeking to transition into commercial real estate.

I know that you are extremely busy; however, I would appreciate 15-20 minutes of your time to connect with you and learn more about your career and experience. Thank you in advance for your time and I hope to hear from you soon.

Regards,
Melissa

Feel free to use this message as a template as you begin to use LinkedIn as a tool to assist you in your career journey. In addition, this template works for emails outside of LinkedIn if you seeking to schedule informational interviews with professionals.

Networking

Networking used to be my least favorite activity. I despised the feeling of walking into a "networking happy hour" and having to strike up conversations with a complete stranger. However, during my unemployment, I used it as an opportunity to market myself and my experience. Also, it was a great way for me to get out of the house. Networking is vital for your professional and personal growth. In my opinion, it's through the connections you make that you're able to gain clarity on your passions and career.

Let's break down what it means to network. Dictionary.com defines it as "an association of individuals having a common interest, formed to provide mutual assistance, helpful information, or the like." It took time for me to understand the mutual assistance part. I mean, what could I offer with no job, limited connections and a tightly budgeted bank account? I continuously walked into events expecting a job, expecting a mentor, or expecting a sales lead. However, here's the thing about networking and relationship building, everyone can smell a selfish vulture from a mile away. I wasn't getting anything out of it because I wasn't willing to give. The same approach I used towards dating and maintaining friendships, I used towards networking. Here are some pointers:

Actively Listen· Be engaged by genuinely listening to the person in front of you. Most people can read your body language, especially if it conveys that you're uninterested. A recent Harvard Business School article by Rebecca Knight states that "standing up straight with your shoulders back helps you come across as confident and commanding; slouching and looking down at your feet has the opposite effect". Be sure to face them, smile and make eye contact. By actively listening, you'll be able to ask relevant questions about the person or what they are discussing. For example, "What made you get into XYZ career? Why do you think there will be another real estate down turn in the next few months? What has your experience been like working for XYZ company?"

Share information that's mutually beneficial· Keep yourself updated on current events, trending topics in your industry, or recent articles/books you've read. Be willing to make connections and introductions for other people. This is how you can add value. Information is power, and the person who has it always wins.

Quality over quantity· Yes, you could talk to every person in the room but would it be productive and would you honestly remember their names? Networking events are typically 2-3 hours long. I aim to create 3-4 meaningful conversations at every event I attend.

Don't force a connection· Let's face it, sometimes the conversation is just painfully awkward. Always be polite and kindly excuse yourself at the right time.

It will take some practice, but with practice comes confidence. And with confidence you'll be able to work any room.

SURVIVAL TIP

Make it a priority to network with your peers as much as you network with professionals in positions you aspire to achieve. Networking vertically is not the only way to grow professionally. Your peers have so much knowledge and resources. Don't miss the opportunity to build relationships laterally with people as you ascend in your career. Be willing to share your experiences, failures, and thoughts that you know may benefit a colleague. It's not always a competition. Your peers most often hold the keys you need to make moves happen.

CHAPTER SIX

THE REINVENTION PLAN

[17] Therefore, if anyone is in Christ, he is a new creation; old things have passed away; behold, all things have become new. **2 Corinthians 5:17 NKJV**

With unemployment comes a lot of free time. You're used to spending eight hours a day at your old job and planning your life with the remaining 16 hours. Now that you're no longer devoting those eight hours to your old employer what do you do now? I knew that this time was an opportunity for me to work on a lot of areas of my life that I was dissatisfied with. From the way that I looked, to the way that I felt and the relationships that I had, I wanted to make improvements.

Depending on the length of your unemployment, there probably won't be another opportunity in your life where you'll have this much uninterrupted time to work on yourself. While you were employed, what areas of your life did you wish you had the time to improve upon? Below are three key areas I feel that every person should strengthen to become a better person on the other side of unemployment.

Spirit

He shall be like a tree planted by the rivers of water, that brings forth its fruit in its season, whose leaf also shall not wither, and whatever he does shall prosper. - **Psalm 1:3 NKJV**

During this time, I had a strong belief that things would work out for my good. I couldn't tell you where it came from, but I know that my self-encouragement was a result of continuously staying plugged into God. Even as I received rejection emails from applications that I submitted; those moments of discouragement were very short in length. I read the Word of God to fill my cup on a daily basis. In addition, my best friends and I established a weekly prayer call. Once a week we discussed the latest news in our lives but most importantly it was a time for us to fellowship, encourage each other and pray together.

Everything in life flows from your belief and the things that you cannot see. Your spirit is important because it guides your relationship with God, your relationship with yourself, and your relationship with other people. Assuming that you were dissatisfied with your previous position, every time you became tired with work your spirit was probably agitated, tired, annoyed, and unenthused, correct? This is because the work that you were doing didn't align with your gifts and talents. Plant yourself into things that are nourishing your spirit. If money weren't an issue what could you see yourself doing for the rest of your life?

Mind

Remember that book you didn't have time to read? Now you have the opportunity to invest in books and resources that will not only expand your knowledge but also challenge you to grow. I've always been an avid reader of personal finance, autobiographies and romance novels. Books have always been a place where I'm free to use my imagination without limits. Our everyday responsibilities tend to create boundaries we deem as "realistic" for our lives. Continuously read materials that enforces the belief that all things are possible. We have the power to create the life that we want.

I believe that one of my biggest hurdles in growing in my career was my confidence. On the outside I seemed like I had it all together, however, I did a very bad job of advocating for myself when it came to my career. I always had an excuse why I couldn't apply for a new role; ask for a raise, or a better opportunity. Then, I came across a book entitled Successful Women Think Differently by Valorie Burton, which ignited a shift in my mindset. Through reading this book and many others, I discovered I had an issue with self-worthiness. I didn't believe I was worthy enough (it can manifest itself as fear, defensiveness, or even passiveness) to attain the things that I said I wanted. Therefore, I didn't position myself because I feared rejection.

As I dug deep into personal habits and thoughts, I began to think differently. And as I began to think differently, I talked differently, I networked differently, and I interviewed differently. Your mind is the compass for your life. Where will you direct it?

Body

The body is a beautiful temple that most of us neglect to take care of. We tend not to eat enough nourishing foods and we rarely get our bodies moving enough. Studies have shown that aside from weight loss and reducing chronic illness, exercise can assist with increased energy levels, relaxation and feeling happier.

There are only so many jobs you could apply for within a day. I went to the gym because changing my body was one of the few things I could control. My doctor had been telling me for some time that I needed to lose a few pounds and here I was with nothing but time. I started to use my physical journey to transform my mind. Each week that I dropped a pound I was also losing some emotional baggage as well. I had the time to craft the body I wanted, and I went from hating the gym to being excited to go. It was my safe place to release all frustration and it became my sanctuary where I'd often prayed. I stepped into the gym with no idea of what I was doing, I just wanted to get moving. During this time, I lost more than 30 pounds and it's the best I've felt in a long time.

There are many inexpensive options to physical fitness. There are low priced gym options with memberships as low at $15 per month. There are fitness packages you can buy on sites such as Groupon or Living Social. Activities such as boxing, pilates, or even fencing are a few of the many options. Try something new and you'd be surprised what you might discover about yourself. If you're looking for free options, you can find workout videos on YouTube and the Nike Training App also has tons of workouts organized by fitness levels. Many of these workouts can be done in the comfort of your home with limited or no equipment.

Turn Your Gifts into Profits

Everyone is not meant for full-time entrepreneurship; however, everyone has the ability to earn money using the talents they already have. My lay off taught me to never rely on one source of income again. I want to discuss two ways to make money.

The first way is to provide a service. Do you know how to do hair? Are you great with photography? Can you plan events? A service is merely the act of doing something for someone and it is a great way to earn extra cash because all a service needs is you. Throughout college, my friends and family have always asked me to assist them with their résumés or interviewing. I never knew it could be a business until a friend of mine kept encouraging me to charge for my services. I wasn't sure I could make money from it, but once I began to market my services the response was extremely positive. I created a career coaching and development business, The Branded Career, focused on branding and developing women of color in the workplace.

Use your skills from your current profession to provide a service. There are many small businesses that are seeking assistance in marketing, accounting, operations, sales and consulting. And the greatest part about this age of technology and social media is that you can start a business with zero to low startup costs. Everything you need is right at your fingertips.

The second way to make money is to sell a product. If you've been blessed with the gift to cook or bake, sell your treats to the public. Are you a beauty enthusiast and create luxurious body butters? Sell it online. Startup costs for physical products may require some capital for materials or inventory, however, I advise to start small and assess the kind of responses you receive. From there you can make changes and scale your business. You can also sell digital products from eBooks, courses and graphic design, just to name a few.

Creating a side hustle or a business is hard work, but the sacrifice is worth knowing that you've created a cushion for yourself in the future. There is an enormous amount of information online that will help you get started and turn your gifts into profits.

Questions for Reflection

Which of the three areas (spirit, mind, or body) will you focus on and why?

What is a product or a service that your friends and family ask you about?

What are some gifts and talents that you think you could monetize?

What are the start-up costs associated with your new venture idea?

CONCLUSION

Thank you so much for investing in yourself and reading this book. I share your pain and confusion, but commitment to creating a better life. View your unemployment as a period of transformation because what you look and feel like when you started will be completely different when it's over. I truly believe that the best is yet to come; however, I need you to believe that for yourself. This will be the time in your life when you'll be able to testify that not only did you survive, but you thrived. I wish you nothing but success in your future endeavors. I will leave you with this final scripture from Luke 1:45 "Blessed is she who has believed that the Lord would fulfill his promises to her."

Be Blessed,

Melissa

ABOUT THE AUTHOR

Melissa is an executive career coach and founder of The Branded Career, a coaching and consulting agency focused on developing and branding diverse millennial talent in the workplace. Melissa is passionately driven to serve women of color and assist them in their careers as they navigate the workplace and the boardroom. The Branded Career's mission is to provide services, programming, and content that empowers professionals and provides companies with resources to develop their talent.

After facing her first job layoff in 2016, in what she considered one of the biggest setbacks in her adult life, she began sharing her experiences with job hunting. She utilized her struggles of facing the unknown by sharing what she branded to be "an accidental survival guide to bouncing back after getting laid off". Her goal is to help her readers and clients put an end to small thinking and walk confidently into their power, brand and dream career!

References

Self-Employment Assistance Program. n.d.
<https://www.labor.ny.gov/seap/>.

Knight, Rebecca. "How to Increase Your Influence at Work."
Harvard Business Review, Harvard Business School Publishing 16 February 2018, hbr.org/2018/02/how-to-increase-your-influence-at-work

Burton, Valorie. Successful Women Think Differently.
Eugene: Harvest House Publishers, 2012.

www.creativemarket.com. n.d.

www.etsy.com. n.d.

www.fiverr.com. n.d.

www.upwork.com. n.d.